Caving

Caving

Exploring Limestone Caves

Larry Dane Brimner

Franklin Watts
A Division of Scholastic Inc.
New York • Toronto • London • Auckland • Sydney
Mexico City • New Delhi • Hong Kong
Danbury, Connecticut

For my Paseo del Sol and Col. Johnston friends in Sierra Vista and Fort Huachuca.

For answering my last-minute questions and providing helpful information, I am grateful to David Elkowitz, Park Ranger at Carlsbad Caverns.

To make sure yours is a safe experience, cave with a minimum of two other experienced cavers, make use of all safety equipment, and use care and common sense. The author and publisher are not responsible for injuries or accidents occurring from any caving activities.

Note to readers: Definitions for words in **bold** can be found in the Glossary at the back of this book.

Photographs ©: Alan Ladd/www.vintageviews.com: 36; Clint Farlinger: 2, 11 top; Corbis-Bettmann: 18, 19 (Richard T. Nowitz); Earth Scenes: 20 (C.C. Lockwood); Kevin Downey Photography: 23 (Urs Widmer), 24, 43; Liaison Agency, Inc.: 46 (Peter Beattie) 30 (Patrice Georges), 50 (Jeff Topping); National Geographic Image Collection: 35 (Stephen L. Alverez), 5 bottom, 14, 15 (Sisse Brimberg), 32, 38 (Joseph H. Bailey & Larry Kinney), cover, 5 top, 8, 11 bottom, 28, 33, 34, 44, 52 (Michael Nichols); Photo Researchers, NY: 13 (Eric & David Hosking), 41 (Didier Jordan), 9 (Charles E. Mohr), 26, 27 (Richard T. Nowitz); Stone: 37 (John & Eliza Forder), 53 (Kerrick James), 21 (Jerry Kobalenko), 16, 17 (A & L Sinibaldi), 6 (Tom Till); Visuals Unlimited: 48, 49 (Albert J. Copley), 12 (E.J. Maruska).

The illustration on the cover shows LeChuguilla Cave, the deepest and fourth-longest cave in the United States at Carlsbad Caverns National Park, New Mexico. The photograph opposite the title page shows calcite formations at Carlsbad Caverns National Park.

Library of Congress Cataloging-in-Publication Data

Brimner, Larry Dane.
  Caving: exploring limestone caves / by Larry Dane Brimner
      p.   cm.— (Watts Library)
  Includes bibliographical references and index.
  ISBN 0-531-20318-2 (lib. bdg.) 0-531-16582-5 (pbk.)
  1. Caving—Juvenile literature. [1. Caving. 2. Caves.] I. Title. II. Series.
GV200.62 .B75   2001
796.52'5—dc21 4-29-08   00-043783

Contents

The opening of a cave, such as the Leviathan opening inside the Worthington Mountains in Nevada, can be incredibly large.

Chapter One

The World of Caves

Beneath the surface of the earth lies a world of awesome beauty. It is the world inside caves. Not all caves are spectacular, but enter the right one, and you'll see an odd and eerie assortment of stone formations found nowhere else on Earth. These cave **phenomena**—for example, soda straws, stone draperies, and cave pearls—have taken thousands of years to form. Their curious beauty remains hidden to all but the intrepid few who venture into the depths to explore them.

Decorating a Cave

Natural cave decorations are called **speleothems**, a term that comes from the Greek words *spelaion*, meaning cave, and *thema*, meaning deposit. Speleothems, or cave deposits, grow over time when water seeps into the cave and deposits minerals that build up drop by drop, granule by granule.

The most common speleothems in limestone caves are **stalactites** and **stalagmites**. Stalactites hang from a cave's ceiling like icicles, while stalagmites grow upward from its floor. (An easy way to remember the difference is to think of the *c* in stalactite as ceiling.) How do these cave marvels develop?

A climber studies the stalactites and stalagmites inside the Carlsbad Caverns National Park.

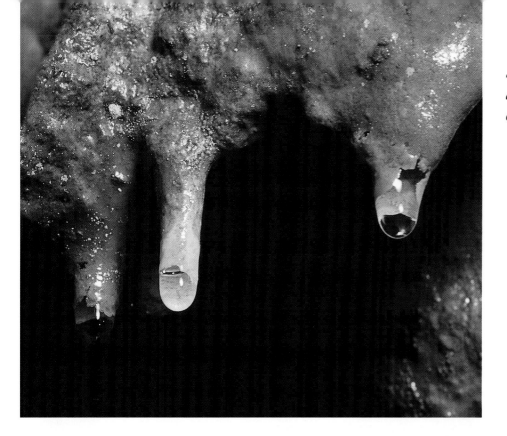

Stalactites form downward from drops of water.

When water bubbles through the soil, it picks up carbon dioxide from decaying plants and animals, and forms a mild acid called **carbonic acid**. Carbonic acid dissolves the cave's limestone, and produces a calcite solution that flows through the cracks and fissures. The solution eventually reaches the ceiling of a cave, where a drop forms. When the drop evaporates, a tiny bit of calcite, the main ingredient of limestone, is left behind. A stalactite begins to form from the calcite. As more water drops form and evaporate, the stalactite grows.

Speleologists, the scientists who study caves, used to think that stalagmites grew much the way a plant grows—from inside the earth outward. Now they know that stalagmites are formed in the same way as stalactites. Many of the drops that

Bit by Bit

How fast does a speleothem grow? It is a slow process. Stalactites grow only about an inch every century.

No Ordinary Straw

Some soda straws grow several feet before breaking off. One of the longest, measured at about 21 feet in length, is in Arizona's Kartchner Caverns.

form on a cave's ceiling are too large to remain suspended. These large drops splash to the cave floor. Here the calcite builds speck by speck until a stalagmite begins to grow toward the ceiling. If the stalactite and stalagmite continue to grow, they will eventually meet and join, and what forms is a column.

Most stalactites are cone-shaped, but this is not the only shape. Unlike regular stalactites, soda straws have hollow, tube-like centers. They form when calcite is deposited in a circular shape. A "straw" or tube grows as the solution flows down the inside of the calcite circle, depositing layer upon layer.

Draperies, another type of stalactite, are translucent sheets of calcite that hang from a cave's ceiling. They resemble the draperies you might find hanging across your living room windows. A drapery forms in the same way as a stalactite. However, if the ceiling is slanted, the solution may trickle over the surface like a tiny stream and deposit calcite in wavy folds and curves. Over time, the folds and curves form sheets of calcite.

Clusters of cave pearls (below) and draperies (above) can be found at Carlsbad Caverns National Park.

Like oyster pearls, cave pearls form around a grain of sand or some other sediment. Forming in pools, cave pearls begin to take shape when calcite clings to the grain. Agitated by water dripping from the ceiling, the calcite pearls remain in constant motion. This motion causes the calcite deposits to take on a rounded, pearl-like appearance.

Cave Visitors and Dwellers

Speleothems are not the only marvels that await cave explorers. Caves provide shelter and protection for an unusual assortment of animal life.

Perhaps the most famous cave animal is the bat. Equipped with **echolocation**, a kind of built-in sonar system, bats emit sounds that bounce off objects. When they hear the echoes,

The Dragon Connection

In seventeenth-century Europe, many people thought the translucent white salamanders found in caves were the young of dragons.

A bat leaves a cave to look for food.

These aurochs, ancestors of domestic oxen, were painted on the walls of Lascaux Cave in France.

they are safely guided through the dark environment of a cave. Many species of bats live in caves. They take shelter, hibernate, and bear and raise their young in the caves. Except during their winter hibernation, they leave the caves nightly to look for food.

Animals that live their whole lives in caves are called **troglodytes**, or cave dwellers. These include some types of flatworms, crayfish, salamanders, shrimp, and beetles. They are blind and colorless. To help them survive in their world of total darkness, cave dwellers may have extended antennae or extrasensitive nerves to find their way around.

Primitive art is another treasure that cavers might find, especially in the caves of France and Spain. One of the most recent finds, the Chauvet Cave near Avignon, France, has more than three hundred images of woolly rhinos, horses, elk, bears, and lions. The images, which some experts believe were painted by spitting pigments made from plants and animal blood upon the rocky surfaces, are more than thirty thousand years old. No one knows why people painted the images and painted within caves. We know only that the creators faced a difficult task when they crawled on their bellies by torchlight to paint them.

Antelope Canyon in Arizona was formed by water.

Chapter Two

How Caves Are Formed

Caves exist in almost every region of the world. How they were formed depends on the material from which they are made.

Wind, Water, and Nature

Sandstone caves, common to the American Southwest, are typically carved by a combination of wind, rain, and water action. They form at the bases of cliffs where the sandstone is not cemented together well. Because sandstone caves are drier than many other types of caves, they often provided shelter in earlier times. The **Anasazis**, an early people who inhabited the Four Corners region of the United States (New Mexico, Arizona, Utah, and Colorado), built elaborate cliff dwellings in the mouths of sandstone caves.

Unlike most other caves, which form slowly over time, lava caves, or tubes, form quickly. When a volcano violently erupts and spews molten lava from its mouth, the lava spills down the volcano's slopes, forming rivers of melted, fiery rock. The outer layer of lava cools and forms a crust when exposed to the air. Beneath the crust, however, molten lava continues to flow. When the eruption is over and the lava drains from beneath the crust, a tubelike cave remains.

Lava tubes may be many miles in length and branch out in several directions. They may contain rooms with ceilings that are 80 feet high or may be so small that a caver must belly-crawl through them. The entrances of lava tubes usually develop when a portion of the crust collapses.

Just as calcite speleothems decorate limestone caves, wondrous formations may decorate lava tubes. Lava-cicles,

decorations that resemble stalactites, may hang from the ceiling. Lava falls, lava flow frozen for all time, may ripple 30 feet down a wall. Since lava rock is very sharp and jagged, special care must be taken when exploring the tubes.

Littoral caves, or sea caves, are usually formed in the same manner as sandstone caves, by water and wind action. Virtually every coastline is dotted with littoral caves. Waves

Rosh Hanikrah Sea Caves in Israel are littoral caves that the Mediterranean Sea formed.

This diver explores the underwater caves at Naharan Cenote Quintana Roo in Mexico.

blast against coastal cliffs and cause the weaker rock to wear away. Eventually shallow caves develop. Littoral caves and their cousins, underwater caves, are potentially the most dangerous types of caves to explore. Tide action has been known to catch littoral cave explorers by surprise, filling the entrance—also the exit—with seawater.

Underwater caves started out as dry caves above sea level before the great ice sheets that blanketed North America and Europe began to melt forty thousand years ago. The melting ice eventually caused the oceans to rise, filling

the dry caves with seawater. These caves are often dangerous to explore because cavers must use diving equipment to get there. If a cave-diver isn't careful, he or she may kick up silt, clouding the way out. Another danger lies in simply running out of oxygen.

Most glacier caves form high in the mountains when melted ice water seeps into cracks in the ice. As it flows through these fractures, the warmed water melts away layers of ice, and the fractures grow in size. Inside a glacier cave the walls are milky white and ice blue, and they become decorated

Some ice caves are massive, as this one on Ellesmere Island, Canada.

with stalactites and stalagmites as dripping water refreezes. Cavers who explore glacier caves do so in the colder months because then the caves are less slushy. They wear warm clothing to protect themselves from exposure to cold temperatures and have a knowledge of mountaineering equipment and technique.

Limestone Caves—Favorites Among Cavers

The giants among caves, and those most commonly explored, are limestone caves. They grow to immense proportions and are sometimes linked by tunnels and passageways to form systems that are hundreds of miles in length.

Limestone is a sedimentary rock that is found all over the world. It is called *sedimentary* because it is made up of sediment, the decayed plants and animals that once covered most of the Earth. Many of these sedimentary areas were thrust up into mountain ranges from various movements of the Earth,

and the pressure brought against the limestone during this upward thrusting left faults and cracks in it.

Areas where limestone caves have formed are called karst lands, named after an area in Croatia and Slovenia that has many limestone caves. The karst process requires two essential ingredients: limestone and water. As mentioned previously in Chapter One, when water comes into contact with limestone, some of the limestone dissolves and forms carbonic

These shells in the limestone are fossils, or the remains of animals from long ago. They make up the sediment in limestone.

The Grandest of Cave Systems

With more than 350 miles of mapped passageways, Kentucky's Mammoth Cave is thought to be the longest cave system in the world—at least three times longer than any other known cave system. Parts of the cave system still remain unexplored. Geologists estimate that there may be as many as 600 miles of yet undiscovered passageways.

Ancient artifacts and human mummies that have been found in Mammoth Cave indicate that people knew about and explored it as early as 4,000 years ago. Over time, however, they forgot about it. In 1798 it was rediscovered by Stephen Bishop (1780–1850), an African-American slave (right). Bishop made extensive maps of the cave's passageways and guided tours through it after the owner opened it to the public.

Bishop's keen familiarity with the cave served another important historic purpose. Bishop was an agent for the Underground Railroad, a secret antislavery movement during the 1800s. Bishop often used the cave's many passageways to hide runaway slaves who were on their way to the North.

acid. Carbonic acid is mildly **corrosive**, meaning that it eats away at limestone.

Limestone caves, then, are formed when water, coming in the form of rain, flows into faults and cracks in the limestone surface. The water dissolves some of the limestone and creates a solution of carbonic acid. The solution, in turn, dissolves even more limestone as it flows to the lowest possible point it can find. Since limestone caves are formed, in part, by a solution of carbonic acid, they are sometimes called solution caves.

Carbonic acid, however, isn't the only factor that forms limestone caves. Underground streams also help broaden and deepen them. When their work is done, the streams either dry up or find another path. This dual action by carbonic acid and underground streams is why limestone caves are the grandest caves of all. Their grandeur offers cave explorers the potential to discover and chart new passageways, even in caves that have been heavily explored. Because of this, limestone caves are favorites with cavers.

A visitor explores Luray Caverns, a show cave, in Virginia.

Chapter Three

Basic Gear

To experience caving, or **spelunking**, at its most elementary, you may want to visit a commercially developed cave, a so-called **show cave**. Show caves give the general public an opportunity to enjoy the wonders of caves without any special equipment, other than comfortable shoes.

A visit to a show cave will unfold the geologic marvels that lie beneath the Earth's surface. It may also ignite your appetite for **wild caves**, and the secrets waiting there. If it does, you'll need more equipment than just comfortable shoes.

"Roughing It" the Show Cave Way

With stairways, paths, and dramatic lighting in show caves and caverns, visitors don't have to crawl through mud or carry their own sources of light. In some cases, they may even be whisked to various levels by elevators and lunch in underground cafeterias!

A Cave's Three Parts

Caves are divided into three parts: the entrance, the twilight zone, and the dark zone. A cave's entrance may be large or small. It may be visible or hidden by dense growth. It may be an opening in the side of a hill or mountain or a pit on the surface of flat land. Cave entrances, and the twilight zone, have long been used as shelter by both people and animals.

Filtered light penetrates into the twilight zone, also called the **variable temperature zone**. Only in the summer is it cooler than at the entrance, and a variety of animals, among them snakes and skunks, may take shelter there to escape the daytime heat. Because there is light, there may also be green plants growing. As you go farther into the twilight zone, however, the light becomes dimmer, and green plants give way to fungi and molds.

The dark zone is—you guessed it—DARK! There is no light here. Hence, there are no green plants. The animals that call the dark zone their home have adapted to their world of darkness. Some of the animals you may find in the dark zone include beetles, fish, salamanders, and spiders. The dark zone, deep within the earth, is a zone of constant temperature. In the dark zone, pools of water and the air remain the same temperature year-round. But the temperature depends upon the cave's altitude and distance from the equator. It is the dark zone that is the most beautiful part of a cave; it is the zone that adventurous cavers seek when they begin their quest.

Getting Ready

To explore a cave entrance, or even the twilight zone, a caver may need relatively little equipment. Often, a light source will be sufficient. Exploring the dark zone is a different story.

A caver, wearing a helmet with many flashlights, prepares himself for a very dark cave.

- **Light**   The most obvious piece of equipment that you need to explore the dark zone is light. Unlike bats, people are not equipped with echolocation! Cavers carry a minimum of three different light sources. The most important of the light sources is attached to the helmet. The other two or more lights are referred to as backup lights and can be hand-held flashlights, battery-operated lamps, or carbide lamps. Carbide is a chemical that produces a gas when combined with water and looks like small pieces of dark, gray gravel.

There are advantages and disadvantages to each type of light source. Batteries are bulky. In a tight situation, such as a narrow passageway, battery-operated lights may hinder your progress and require removal before you can advance farther into the cave. They are also heavy, an issue if you plan to make lengthy cave visits.

Scorched Seat Syndrome

Another disadvantage to carbide lamps is what some cavers call "scorched seat syndrome"—when one caver follows too closely behind another and the lamp burns the caver in front.

Carbide flames, on the other hand, will burn for about four hours. Extra carbide must be carried so that a carbide lamp can be refueled. The extra carbide must be carried in a water-tight container. Any contact with water, whether the carbide is in the lamp or not, will result in the production of acetylene gas. The gas may ignite from the slightest spark. Carbide flame lamps are also prone to breakdowns, so most cavers who rely on them carry a small repair kit and replacement parts. Another important consideration is that carbide residue— what is left behind after carbide is used in a lamp—is extremely toxic and must be carried back out of the cave.

What are the advantages? Battery-operated lamps are simple to operate, but some people argue that using a carbide flame creates a brighter light. Others say that many electric lights produce more light than carbide. In the end, the decision is yours. Ask around before you make a purchase. More experienced cavers will gladly share their insights and preferences with you.

- **Helmet** A helmet is NOT an optional piece of equipment. One with a light should be worn at all times when caving as it will protect your head from falling debris and any unnoticed sharp rocks. It must include a chin strap, otherwise

the helmet could fall from your head when you're climbing and possibly cause injury to someone below. A plastic hard hat is not adequate. Outfitting shops sell helmets specifically designed for cavers.

- **Gloves and Pads**   Gloves will protect your hands from sharp, jagged rocks, and they will prevent rope burn if you are doing any rope work. Most cavers use soft, unlined leather gloves. Pads—either the kind that skateboarders wear or those found in garden supply shops—will protect the knees of your caving coveralls. They are bulky, but they will save wear and tear on your outer clothing. Some cavers recommend sewing leather patches over the knees of your outer clothing in lieu of the bulky pads.

• **Rope** Caves exist in two dimensions, horizontal and vertical, and some are a combination of the two. Cavers have to rely on rope work to get them to certain parts of some caves. Vertical caving requires specialized techniques and equipment, and is only performed by very experienced cavers.

Most cavers rely on rope that uses nylon kermantle construction. In other words, the rope consists of a core (kern) and a braided cover (mantle). This produces a rope of considerable strength and durability. Unlike rock-climbing ropes, which are dynamic and stretch to absorb the impact of a fall, caving ropes are designed for minimal stretch.

To keep your rope in topnotch condition, be sure to keep it dry and out of sunlight. Inspect it with your eyes and fingers before each expedition. If you notice any frays or lumps upon inspection, replace it. Also, keep your rope away from

This caver coils a 600-foot-long caving rope that will support 8,000 pounds.

A photographer, held up by a harness, takes pictures inside a cave.

chemicals. Battery acid can destroy the core without visual appearance. A rope is your lifeline. You want to be certain you can depend on it.

• **Harness** Today most cavers rely on harnesses to lower themselves into caves. Made from wide, nylon webbing, a harness fits snugly around the waist and thighs. Since harnesses vary, be sure to follow the manufacturer's instructions for tying in to, or attaching, your rope.

• **Carabiners** A carabiner, or biner (pronounced "beaner"), is an aluminum alloy or steel link with a locking gate. A biner is used to make connections, usually between the caver's rope and something else, such as the harness.

Wearing a helmet, boots, and knee pads, a caver sorts his gear connected to many carabiners during a climb in Snail Shell Cave in Borneo, East Malaysia.

Going Down

When Jim White (1882–1946) decided to explore the deeper reaches of Carlsbad Caverns (New Mexico) in the early 1900s, harnesses had yet to be invented. Instead, he rigged up a bucket that was used for collecting bat guano, or fertilizer, from the cave to make the descent.

- **Descenders**   The key to making a controlled drop into a cave versus an uncontrolled and rapid drop is a device called a descender. A descender has one job, and that is to control the flow of the rope. To do this, it employs the principle of friction. Friction acts like a braking mechanism by creating drag on the rope, and this allows the caver to drop or abseil at a safe speed. **Abseiling**, as descending is correctly called, relies on making a controlled descent down a fixed rope.

There are several varieties of descenders to choose from: figure eights, racks, and bobbins, to name but three. The type you eventually adopt for use will be determined by experience and, probably, the influence of your caving buddies.

• **Ascenders** Once you abseil, or rope down, into a cave, you eventually need to get back up. You could climb the rope hand-over-hand and use strength to make your ascent, but most cavers use ascenders. You'll need two (and maybe three, depending on your rigging).

Ascenders, or jammers, slide up the rope in one direction. Then ratchet devices, which are usually spring operated, lock them in place and prevent them from slipping back down the rope.

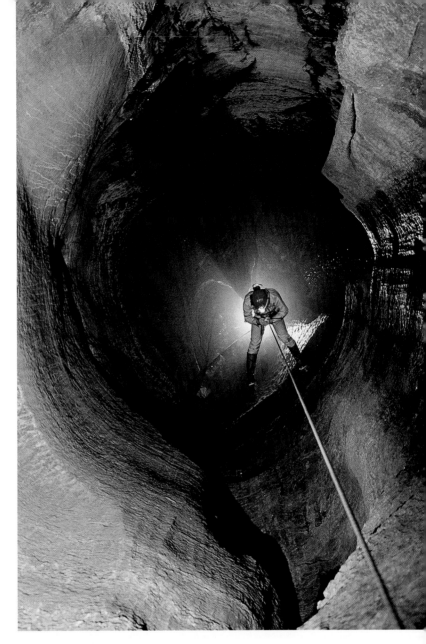

A caver abseils down Notts Pot Cave in England.

Today's cavers use modern technology to make cave exploration more accessible and safe. This technology, however, comes with a price. Caving is not an inexpensive sport.

This young caving group sits in a low cave, holding carbide lamps, which they have detached from their helmets.

Chapter Four

Safe Caving

As with any activity, caving presents a potential for injury. You can reduce the risks with training. We learn best from those who know what they're doing. Join a caving group. Many local colleges and universities have outing groups and are receptive to beginning spelunkers. Some chapters of the Sierra Club sponsor outings as well as YMCAs and scouting groups. You might also contact the National Speleological Society (NSS) and inquire about your local chapter. An advantage to beginning with a group, aside from acquiring their skill and advice, is that most will share their equipment with you while you decide if caving is something you want to pursue.

If you live near or plan to visit an area known for its caves, check with the local visitors' bureau to find out if classes for beginners are offered. Many areas of karst lands try to maximize their tourist potential by offering half-day and full-day outings. The outings are led by experienced guides, and reliable equipment is usually included in the fee.

Ultimately, experience is the key to safe caving.

Dress the Part

There are other steps you can take to make sure an outing is safe and comfortable. The first of these is to dress the part. In addition to the caving gear mentioned in the last chapter, you'll want to wear warm, sturdy clothing. Shorts and T-shirts are inappropriate, except for a minimum exposure in the warmest, driest of caves.

Hypothermia, a condition where the body loses more heat than it generates, is one of the greatest threats to cavers. In severe cases of hypothermia, the victim, if untreated, simply freezes to death. To avoid hypothermia on an outing of several hours, layer your clothing. Most cavers today wear underclothing made of polypropylene. It's the same material that skiers wear under their ski outfits. It will keep you warm and dry. Thermal underwear is a suitable alternative. Cavers who are familiar with a cave will be able to make recommendations about appropriate clothing.

The Cavers' Motto

The cavers' motto is, "Take nothing but pictures. Leave nothing but footprints. Kill nothing but time."

Over the undergarments, cavers wear zippered coveralls made of rugged denim or the same durable nylon material used for backpacks. Zippers are preferred over buttons because they will help keep out the mud and won't snag on rocks. It is recommended that you carry a change of dry clothing in your pack.

Many people wear sneakers on their first few outings. While sneakers are comfortable in the beginning, they don't offer the support and protection that your feet need for extended caving. Ankle-high boots will protect your feet from cold and abrasion. The standard in caving today is boots with light-colored soles. Why? Boots with black or dark soles can leave behind scuff marks.

Be sure your boots fit snugly. Loose-fitting boots may produce blisters. Snug boots worn with a pair of athletic socks against the skin and wool socks over those will keep your feet dry and lessen the chance of blisters forming.

Cavers must wear protective undergarments and overgarments when exploring a cave.

Use Your Head

The right choice in clothing will keep you reasonably comfortable in the cave environment. In case a mishap occurs, however, be certain that your party is carrying a first-aid kit and be familiar with what to do. If you haven't taken a first-aid class, enroll in one. Your local YMCA or Red Cross may be good places to start. At least one member of your caving party should be familiar with first-aid practices. If more know first aid, that's even better. Also, each person should have a compass (and know how to use it), four plumber's candles, and waterproof matches. In an emergency, candles can provide light and warmth. When underground, use your head. Think before you act. Caving is meant to be a fun, enjoyable adventure. With a little attention to details and some thought, it can be just that.

Caving Guidelines

- Don't cave alone. Go in a party of three or more, with at least two members being experienced adult cavers.
- Be aware of the weather. Some caves are subject to flooding. They are the last place you want to be if a storm is predicted.
- Always inform another person where you are going and when you expect to return, and stick to the plan.
- Never "free" climb. Climb only with the aid of a rope.
- Never use alcohol and/or drugs before entering a cave.
- Don't play practical jokes, as they may put you or another person at risk.

Graffiti can destroy the beauty of a cave.

The Caving Code

There was a time, before people became aware that their actions could impact the environment, when people would thoughtlessly discard rubbish into the mouths of caves. Cave explorers thought little about breaking off a soda straw for a souvenir, carving their initials into a stalagmite to leave behind evidence of their exploration, or tossing a few pennies into a pool for good luck. Today, we know those actions are selfish and harmful. All cave explorers deserve to see caves in their natural beauty—without graffiti or litter or missing parts.

After removing her shoes, a caver steps lightly barefoot into a clear pool of water inside a cave. She takes great care not to damage or disturb the cave environment.

Modern cave enthusiasts know that caves must be pre-served in their natural state. Aside from offering the visitor amazing sights, they serve a purpose. They are part of the **aquifer system**. An aquifer is a natural, underground reser-voir which ultimately supplies drinking water to homes and irrigation water to farms. Caves channel surface water into aquifers. When we preserve and protect our caves, we also preserve and protect our water.

Caving opens up a new world filled with age-old beauty. A responsible caver will respect that world and preserve it for future generations of cavers and cave enthusiasts.

Lake Cave in Western Australia

Chapter Five

Finding Caves

Caves exist in every part of the world. There are more than two hundred caves in the United States that are open to the general public. Although you won't be able to explore show caves—such as Wind Cave (South Dakota), Mammoth Cave (Kentucky), and Luray Caverns (Virginia)—in the same way you might a wild cave, a visit will introduce you to their many wonders. The Jenolan region of Australia, near Sydney, boasts an estimated three hundred caves, several of which are show caves open to the public. Also, guided tours, common to most show caves, will better acquaint you with the cave-making process. Local chambers of commerce and tourism boards are good places to begin your search. They can provide you with information about local caving attractions, especially if caves in the region are commercial ventures.

The Wild Side

If you are like many people, show cave tours will eventually feel limiting. You will begin to hear the call to explore caves that are not commercial, or caves that are not shared with the general public. You'll want to belly-crawl into regions that less spirited souls would never dream of visiting for some serious spelunking.

Your local chapter of the National Speleological Society will be able to tell you about local caving destinations. The NSS is an organization that is affiliated with the American

These cavers explore a cave by canoe to study its mysteries.

A Secret Revealed

In 1974, Randy Tufts and Gary Tenen discovered a **live cave**—meaning water was still percolating through it and forming speleothems—on property owned by the Kartchner family in the Whetstone Mountains near Sierra Vista, Arizona. At first, Tufts and Tenen kept quiet about their discovery, but in 1978 they revealed their find to the Kartchners. Thus began one of the longest kept secrets in caving. For fourteen years, knowledge of Kartchner Caverns, as the cave is now called, was kept to a small circle of friends.

Tufts and Tenen, along with the Kartchners, eventually realized the caverns were too special not to share with others. The property was turned over to the state, and in 1988, the Arizona legislature approved the creation of Kartchner Caverns State Park, which opened to the public in 1999.

Now a show cave that balances commercial venture with preservation, it is hoped that its state park status will protect it so it can be enjoyed by future generations of cave enthusiasts.

Association for the Advancement of Science, and it was formed to locate, study, and conserve caves. Local chapters meet often to share information and experiences. Although caving is mostly an adult sport, here you will meet experienced cavers who will be happy to introduce young people to the sport and to some of their favorite local haunts. Although they are usually a close-knit group, members share information about their favorite caves and new finds with other like-minded enthusiasts.

Most caves are privately owned. Because of this, you will have to receive permission from the property owner to enter them. Many are obliging, but some have been put off by discourteous cavers who have been rude or have not shown respect for private property. Others have become weary of picking up litter left by thoughtless visitors.

When you seek permission to explore a cave on private property, ask where your group can leave its vehicles so they won't be in the way and stay on established paths. In short, be a caving diplomat. If permission to enter the property is denied, respect that decision as well.

The Caver's Notebook

As you become more involved in caving, you'll soon discover that there's more to an outing than simply exploring a cave. Most cavers feel it is their obligation to chart a cave's passageways or to sketch a cave's formations. These records offer

Cavers like to keep a journal or diary, writing notes or charting maps of their cave explorations.

more than memories. Like a map, a caver's notebook entries may chart the course for generations of future cave explorers.

Every year new caves are discovered, and caves thought to have been fully explored reveal new passageways. Lucky the caver who first charts a discovery—and gets to name it!

A kayaker explores Emerald Cave in Black Canyon on the Colorado River in Arizona.

Glossary

abseiling—descending, or going down, into a cave

Anasazis—an ancient people who once inhabited cliff dwellings in the Four Corners area of New Mexico, Colorado, Arizona, and Utah

aquifer system—a natural, underground reservoir that supplies drinking and irrigation water

carbonic acid—a mild acid formed when carbon dioxide, a product from decaying plants and animals, dissolves in water

corrosive—something, such as acid, which is capable of wearing away something else

echolocation—a natural, built-in sonar system that enables bats to navigate by sending out sounds and listening for their echoes

hypothermia—a serious condition where the body loses more heat than it generates

littoral caves—sea caves found in coastal cliffs

live cave—a cave that is still forming and evolving through the seepage of water

phenomena—things that are unusual and remarkable

show cave—a cave commercially developed for tourists

speleologists—scientists who study caves

speleothems—cave decorations made by mineral deposits

spelunking—the exploration of caves and caverns

stalactites—mineral deposits that form on the ceilings of caves

stalagmites—mineral deposits that form on the floors of caves

troglodytes—animals that spend their entire lives in caves

variable temperature zone—the twilight zone of a cave, that part where the temperature fluctuates

wild cave—a cave in its natural state

To Find
Out More

Books

Gibbons, Gail. *Caves and Caverns.* San Diego, CA: Harcourt Brace & Co., 1993.

Gurnee, Russell H. *Gurnee Guide to American Caves.* Teaneck, NJ: Zephyrus Pess, 1980.

Jacobson, Don, and Lee Stral. *Caves and Caving.* Boyne City, MI: Harbor House Publishers, 1986.

Judson, David, ed. *Caving Practice & Equipment.* Leicester, England: British Cave Research Association/Cordee, 1995.

Pinney, Roy. *The Complete Book of Cave Exploration.* New York: Coward-McCann, Inc., 1962.

Schultz, Ron. *Looking Inside Caves and Caverns*. Santa Fe, NM: John Muir Publications, 1993.

Silver, Donald M. *One Small Square: Cave*. New York: W.H. Freeman & Company, 1993.

Silverman, Sharon Hernes. *Going Underground: Your Guide to Caves in the Mid-Atlantic*. Philadelphia: Camino Books, Inc., 1991.

Online Sources

Carlsbad Caverns National Park
http://www.carlsbad.caverns.national-park.com/
This site has information about the history of Carlsbad Caverns, as well as information about activities and tours.

The Cave Page
http://www.cavepage.magna.com.au/cave/
This site offers articles about caving in Australia and Europe plus links to other caving websites.

Kartchner Caverns State Park
http://www.pr.state.az.us/parkhtml/kartchner.html
This site details the discovery and long-kept secret of Kartchner Caverns, as well as information about tours.

Mammoth Cave National Park
http://www.nps.gov/maca/home.htm
This site reveals everything there is to know about Mammoth Cave, from its discovery to current maps of its passageways.

Organizations

American Cave Conservation Association
P.O. Box 409
Horse Cave, KY 42749
http://www.cavern.org
This group is dedicated to the conservation of caves and ground water supplies through education.

The National Speleological Society
2813 Cave Avenue
Huntsville, AL 35810
http://www.caves.org
The purpose of this club is to find, study, and preserve caves.

Sierra Club
85 Second Avenue, 2nd Floor
San Francisco, CA 94105
http://www.sierraclub.org
This organization promotes the enjoyment and conservation of the natural environment.

A Note on Sources

When I research any topic, I think it is important to gather as many sources as possible. If I am personally unfamiliar with the topic, my first stop is the children's room of a good local library. Children's books, I've discovered, have a remarkable way of distilling information and making it clear. Thus armed with a basic knowledge of the topic, I then read as many technical books by experts and authorities as possible. For this particular book, my search led me to David Judson's *Caving Practice & Equipment*, Roy Pinney's *The Complete Book of Cave Exploration*, and Sharon Hernes Silverman's *Going Underground: Your Guide to Caves in the Mid-Atlantic*. I also keep alert to articles in newspapers and magazines. Online articles, such as "Cave Creatures Endangered" by Lee Dye for ABCNews.com, which suggested that compromised cave systems might spell trouble for our aquifers, help fill in any gaps.

I also gain knowledge about a topic by speaking with experts and practitioners in the field. Typically, people are eager to share knowledge of their specialized fields, and this information often adds a human touch to my topic. When the topic lends itself, I become a doer. Firsthand experience and observation give me a sense of what a topic is all about and, I believe, lend credibility to my books. I have been lucky enough to see stalactites in Carlsbad Caverns, soda straws in Kartchner Caverns, and Anasazi ruins in the cliffs at Mesa Verde National Park in Colorado.

—*Larry Dane Brimner*

Index

Numbers in *italics* indicate illustrations.

About the Author

Larry Dane Brimner has been an elementary, junior high, and high school teacher, as well as a teacher-trainer at San Diego State University. Among his more than seventy-five books for young people are several Franklin Watts titles, including these others about sports: *Mountain Biking*, *Surfing*, *Rock Climbing*, and *Snowboarding*, an IRA/CBC "Children's Choice" book. His research has put him on inline skates and taken him up rock faces, but he has never belly-crawled through a wild cave!